Dedication

"Je dédie ce livre a tous les hommes Américains qui pensent avec leur cerveau, pas avec leur bite."

(I dedicate this book to all American men who think with their brain, not with their dicks.)

THE FRENCH CONNECTIONS PUBLISHING

The French Connections Publishing:
www.thefrenchperspective.com

ISBN: 979-8-218-05358-1 (paperback)
ISBN: 979-8-218-05359-8 (ebook)

Ordering Information:
Special discounts are available on quantity purchases by corporations, associations, and others. For details, contact guyblaise@thefrenchperspective.com

Table of Contents

love
like a
man

A FRENCHMAN'S GUIDE TO HELP AMERICAN MEN BE BETTER PARTNERS

GUY BLAISE

Before You Say I Do

Gentlemen, I regret to inform you that the women in your lives are not happy. You take better care of your vehicles than your relationships. You know more about what is under the hood of your car than you do about how to make a woman orgasm. We all know the old mantra recited to women and by women all across the globe, "You can't change him." The good news is that a man can change himself—if he chooses.

In my last book *Love Like the French*, I answered letters from American women seeking advice on a myriad of relationship topics. Armed with so much insight from their experiences, and based on my personal experiences dating American women, it felt like a book aimed at young couples considering the prospect of marriage or those who have recently married was needed. While my focus is on topics that women care about, the answers apply to men.

This book is not a trial for men. It should serve as a guide to help you become the man that your partner desires and deserves. You may not appreciate everything I have to say, and not every subject will be about you, but by all means take whatever information resonates with you and apply it. I have heard women say, "He's a good guy, but he's just not a good husband/boyfriend." There is no reason why a good man can't also become a good partner. It begins with commitment and is sustained through compromise and communication. A relationship is a journey of experiences, both good and bad.

You will want to keep reading if you recognize yourself in any of the following:

- Men who cannot handle a woman who speaks her mind

- Men who only offer sex in place of support

- Men who are nice but terrible in bed

- Men who are self-centered and emotionally unavailable

- Men with no ambition, no future goals

- Men who flaunt their possessions because they lack a personality

- Men who lie

Set your pride aside for this one. Reflect on your past experiences and consider all of the things that could have been handled differently, resulting in a different outcome. Women are telling us what they want. We simply have to be willing to listen. Every topic in this book was brought to the table by a woman. You may not find the answers to all of your questions, but you can use other men's mistakes to help you become the partner every woman wants. If you are not ready to make a commitment but are seeking a relationship, the Dos and Don'ts section in this book will help you avoid the common mistakes that men make on dating sites.

In Sickness and in Health

Dear Guy,

My fiancée and I are both 25. She was diagnosed with MS eight months after we became engaged. Her health is declining, and I am questioning my ability to care for her and to proceed with the marriage. Is it fair to me to marry her, knowing that she will not be the same person I fell in love with?

-Jonathan, 25

Dear Jonathan,

Sorry to hear about your fiancée. I know the level of stress that a life-threatening illness can create in a relationship. You said "fiancée," meaning you think of her as a lifelong partner. Don't be intimidated by the challenges. We have a French saying, "You have to cultivate your inner elegance." We are referring not only to style, but also to our behavior and treatment of others.

A study done in the U.S. in 2009[1] looked at how often heterosexual couples split due to illness: sadly, it concluded that men tend to leave their partners six times more often than women.[2] It's not easy to commit to life at 25 and carry such a weight on your shoulders, but it's not impossible. When I was your age, I removed the word "Never" from my vocabulary. We are what we think.

I would not encourage you to be one of those men who give up and run away. If you made her your fiancée, I presume you did so because you love her. If you stopped loving her when she became ill, then you were not truly in love in the first place. When we love someone, our instinct is to help them when they are sick or hurt. There are men who do not see the disease but the being. Be one of them. To be her pillar and sun, please cook meals for both of you if she can't, and attend her doctors' appointments with her.

Strength is measured by your ability to endure and cope with challenges. Showing loyalty in times of illness is a great quality. If you decide to move on, be honest with her, she deserves the truth.

Best of luck,

Guy

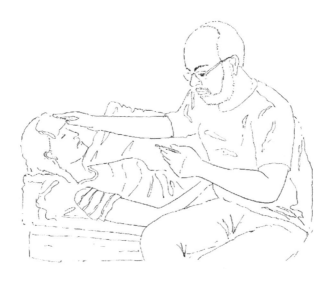

Il n'y a pas d'amour, il n'y a que des preuves d'amour.

—Pierre Reverdy[3]

("There is no love; there is only proof of love.")

How Was Your Day?

Dear Guy,

We have been married for three years. My husband is often in a bad mood after work—a simple question about his day seems to get on his nerves. He says he doesn't want to talk about it and that I should be more understanding. Is this typical male behavior?

- Denise & Matthew

Dear Denise and Matthew,

Thank you for your letter. If you are living together, you certainly know each other's characters. After work, we all carry hours of stories—good and bad—in our heads. Some people choose to vent their frustrations on their partner or have a drink after work. Others prefer silence and isolation.

I used to get upset after work and stay in a bad mood at home on my days off. When I look back, I realize that I spent time being upset about things that I could not control at work—I could not fix someone else's incompetence. Everyone is entitled to a few moments of solitude after a long day at work. This is not, however, a green light to be rude to our partners.

Over the years, I readjusted my attitude and left my work frustrations at work. From time to time, when I felt the mustard rising in my nose (a French expression meaning anger building inside me) and felt overwhelmed by emotions, I found that the best remedy was physical activity. This works for women, too. Perhaps you can participate in an activity as a couple.

Remember, when you get off work, you are not going to a war zone. You don't want to argue with your wife. An angry woman is a stinging wasp. Differences can be resolved peacefully.

A wife asking her husband about his day is a good sign. When she stops caring about his day is the day that he should be concerned.

Best wishes,

Guy

Les ingrédients d'une bonne relation:
l'honnêteté, la confiance, la constance et le respect mutuel.

—Mouctar Keïta[4]

("The ingredients of a good relationship:
honesty, trust, consistency and mutual respect.")

Mister Iceberg

Some of you have two faces: You're a funny guy outside among your friends and family, but an extremely cold husband at home. For example, you might be a guy who is married to his sofa, caressing his remote control, and having a conversation with his television. For you, a wife is an ornament or a housekeeper. For those of you who lack creativity, you are managing to create irreversible chaos. Going to the theater, enjoying movies, relaxing at the beach, and hiking are activities that couples do together to bring oxygen to the relationship. Oxygen is the key to keeping a relationship alive. If you only seem to have fun outside of your home—without your partner—then you don't need a partner in your life. And if you don't, then be honest and tell her so. Don't stay with her for the wrong reasons.

Il ne faut pas regretter la franchise.
L'homme a deux visages est insupportable.

—G. Blaise

("We should not regret honesty.
A man with two faces is unbearable.")

No Boys Allowed

Dear Guy,

My husband is addicted to video games. He gets home from work and plays until dinnertime, then he plays after dinner, sometimes until long after I have gone to bed. He rarely helps with our two children and I am exhausted from having to do everything. I feel like a single mother of three. Should I give him an ultimatum?

- Heather, VA

Dear Heather,

Ultimatums rarely work. A man must know how to balance responsibility with fun. A woman can't feel confident in her relationship when she feels like a parent to her man instead of a partner. It is clear that your husband's behavior is causing you resentment and unhappiness. A dialog is important. I don't know how well you have communicated your feelings to him. It is possible that he is dismissing your complaints as nagging. Perhaps he is not aware of the seriousness of the problem. If he is aware, however, and is continuing the same pattern of behavior, he is making a statement. Ultimately, you cannot change his behavior, but you can decide whether or not you are willing to accept it. After making your feelings clear, you will have to decide if it's game over.

All the best,

Guy

L'homme qui refuse de gérer ses responsabilités est aussi inutile que la bite d'un prêtre.

–G. Blaise

("A man refusing to take responsibilities is as useless as a priest's cock.")

Emotions Have No Gender

Say what you want about the French, but it wouldn't hurt you to be a little more like us when it comes to expressing your emotions. Emotions are not exclusive to one gender, and French men know this. It does not make you less of a man to tell your partner your genuine feelings—it makes you human.

Try it. You may be surprised to find that your improved communication makes your relationship stronger.

Les sentiments sont comme un parachute.
Il ne fonctionne que lorsqu'il est ouvert.

—G. Blaise

("Feelings are like parachutes.
They only work when opened.")

Cock Blockers

I notice many American men staying in relationships out of convenience, knowing they have no intention of marrying their partner. If you know she wants to get married and you do not plan on asking her to marry you, stop wasting her time. Some of you treat your partners like housekeepers and cooks. You behave like roommates who help each other out with bills. Cock blockers get into relationships with women and keep them from seeing other men, even though they are not going to take things to the next level. Men stay in these relationships to kill time until the right one comes along. It is selfish behavior and it says a lot about you. You would never string along someone who truly loves you.

Ne joue pas avec les sentiments d'une femme, le roue tourne.
Aujourd'hui tu joues, demain tu seras le jouet.

—G. Blaise

("Don't play with a woman's feelings. The wheel always turns.
Today you play; tomorrow, you will be the toy.")

The "L" Word

Dear Guy,

I have been with my girlfriend for three months. Is it too soon to say I love you?

- Quincy

Dear Quincy,

I am a big lover. If I had a dollar for every time I said "I love you" to a woman, I would be rich. That does not mean things always went well.

If it feels right, say it. Unfortunately, there is no formula for love. To find out if she loves you back, you have to dare to take the plunge. I have said the "L" word during the first intimate relationship with a lover, if it is deliberate and sincere, I don't need to grit my teeth to say the words. As long as you mean what you say and you are not using it as a manipulation tactic, the time to say it is completely up to you.

I found out over the years that some women are extremely cautious. I had a lover who said "I love you" first, then apologized for saying so. She explained to me later that she wanted to say it quickly, but was afraid of scaring me away.

Your girlfriend is not obligated to say "I love you" when you do. There are no rules that say she has to have the same feelings as you at the same moment. If she doesn't say it back, don't be offended. She may want to get to know you better or may want the relationship to grow before she is ready to take things to that level. You don't have to ask her how she feels. Give her time and she will let you know.

Je t'aime est en relation amoureuse ce qu'est le thermomètre en médecine.
Sans lui, on ne se rendrait jamais exactement compte de la gravité de notre fièvre.

—G. Blaise

("I love you in a relationship is what the thermometer
is in medicine.
Without it, we would never be fully aware of the seriousness
of our fever.")

Bathroom Etiquette

Dear Guy,

My wife is constantly complaining that I am being messy in the bathroom. Is this what women like to nag about after getting married?

- Ted, TX

Dear Ted,

There is no nice way to say this. If you walk into a clean bathroom, piss into the wind, then go about your business without a care in the world, you are creating a conflict with your partner. Whether or not you wash your hands before leaving the bathroom is anyone's guess. If you can't pee properly, I can't imagine you making love right.

Having spoken to many women, I've often heard sharp and repeated criticism about men and the toilet bowls. I personally became aware of it in public bathrooms, which made me more self-aware at home.

Remembering to put the seat up is great, but it is not a green light to douse the toilet with urine. A simple internet search for urinal targets will result in a wide choice of decals that will improve your aim. Practice makes you better. Yes, they are for children, but don't let that deter you if you need the help. And remember—it would only take an extra minute of your day to clean up after yourself should you miss the bullseye. If you put up the seat, remember to put it back down when you're done. Don't give your wife more reason to be disgusted by your lack of cleanliness.

The solution I suggest is to develop a reflex for checking the bathroom before leaving it. Alternatively, like women, you could urinate sitting down to avoid dispersion. It will not make you less of a man. There is a rumor in France suggesting that men who pee sitting down empty their bladders better, which helps prevent prostate issues.

I was an engineer at one point of my life. When I walk into a clean bathroom, Newton's third law of motion[5] comes to mind. To paraphrase: Something that falls from above falls with a penetrating force, therefore it causes water to splash out. To avoid the splashing, I aim for the ceramic. My logic is simple—if you play darts, to avoid hitting the side, you aim at the center. Do the opposite when peeing. There are two benefits to my strategy; you avoid the splashing and you pee in a silent mode. Not all women like to hear the loud noise of a piss storm.

I hope this helps.

Best wishes.

Si tu veux controler tes urines, commence par controler ton penis.

—G. Blaise

("If you want to control your urine, start by controlling your penis.")

Wives in Bad Marriages

A handsome face is not enough. Some men have no idea that their wives are unhappy. I have interviewed many unhappy wives who stay in the marriage for the children, for fear of being alone, the stigma of divorce, or a lack of finances. Being the breadwinner does not automatically make a man a good husband. There is more effort needed than just paying the bills. It is far too easy to fall into a rut and go through the motions of our daily lives. How often do you smile at each other or laugh together? Consider how often you have sex and how attentive you are to her needs in bed.

As a man, I want to know that my partner is happy. I believe that positive energy brings two people together. Every relationship is unique. You will have to communicate and ask difficult questions. Being in tune with your partner and showing appreciation for each other is the best way to avoid a surprise ending.

Le mariage est la seule guerre durant laquelle vous dormez avec votre ennemi.

—Pythagoras[6]

("Marriage is the only war where you sleep with your enemy.")

Excessive Drinking

A few beers on the weekend, a glass of wine with dinner—alcohol is good from time to time. But excessive alcohol is not good for anyone. Many of you are in denial about your alcoholism. According to the National Institute on Alcohol Abuse and Alcoholism, an estimated 95,000 people (approximately 68,000 men and 27,000 women) die from alcohol-related causes annually, making alcohol the third-leading preventable cause of death in the United States.[7] Some of you become verbally abusive when you drink and the ones who suffer the wrath of your slurred, hateful words are those closest to you—your family.

I am aware that alcoholism is a terrible disease and I have a lot of sympathy for those who are struggling. We have heard it many times before; admitting you have a problem is the first step.

If you can't go a day without a drink, it may be time to do some self-reflection. Your loved ones may be tolerating your unacceptable behavior. It is time that you love them back the way they deserve to be loved—by getting help and making changes.

Plus d'hommes se sont noyés dans l'alcool que dans la mer.

—W.C. Fields[8]

("More men have drowned in alcohol than at sea.")

Erection Goes to Pot

Dear Guy,

I am 29 years old and have been smoking weed, cigarettes, and vaping and for about seven years now. My new girlfriend has been frustrated because I struggle to keep my erection. Do you think smoking could be the problem?

- Brian, NM

Dear Brian,

Your letter brought back memories for me. I tried cigarettes when I was a teenager and did not like them. And I recall being invited by my friend Denise who hosted a party at her house every Friday night where everyone smoked pot. Denise convinced me to give it a try. I tried it and it didn't do anything for me. But I can describe what I witnessed among our friends. As the music and smoking went on, I witnessed some euphoria and everyone slowly falling asleep on the couch. Some were acting like kids and telling bad jokes. They all claimed that alcohol is worse than smoking marijuana.

According to the CDC, about 12.5% of American adults smoke cigarettes[9] and 18% of Americans smoke marijuana.[10] Several medical studies link cigarettes with worsening erectile dysfunction,[11] and recent studies have suggested cannabis may negatively impact male fertility.[12] However, the effects of marijuana use on male reproductive processes is still a relatively little-known topic that researchers acknowledge needs more data[13,14] with one 2019 Harvard study actually finding higher concentrations of sperm in men who have smoked marijuana compared with men who have not.[15]

I would suggest that you decrease the frequency of smoking as a "test" to see if you can regain your erection. You should ask your doctor about smoking weed and having children. Lazy sperm syndrome exists.

I am not sure if weed affects sperm production. I do know that Bob Marley smoked marijuana as a spiritual rite and still had many children.

There was a time when infertility was blamed solely on women. Today, we know better. You must find a solution as soon as possible before your girlfriend finds a solution for you.

Le pénis est le plus capricieux des organes.
C'est une corde inutile quand elle choisit de ne pas fonctionner
correctement.

—G. Blaise

("The penis is the most capricious of organs.
It's a useless rope when it chooses not to work correctly.")

Take Initiative

Married men often talk badly about marriage in the company of other men. Guised as a joke, they say to their single friends contemplating marriage *don't do it*. Rather than succumb to an unfulfilling relationship, take some initiative to spice things up.

Seriously, if you want to have a beautiful evening with your wife, make a reservation at a nice restaurant. I am assuming that you know her favorite color, her favorite foods, her likes and dislikes. The occasional pampering doesn't make sense if your wife is always the one initiating and making the arrangements. Schedule a sitter for the kids, reserve your table in advance, arrange for the restaurant to bring out a gift box with dessert; don't wait for a special occasion to do something nice. Be the planner once in a while. Do your part in keeping the romance alive. When you love each other, you take turns demonstrating love and appreciation.

Quand dans une initiative, la volonté rencontre la conviction, la réussite devient une illumination.

—Djarra Moussa Soumanou[16]

("When initiative meets convictions, success becomes enlightenment.")

Men and Condoms

Shopping in Paris in *Le Roi de la Capote* ("The King of Condoms"), I smiled while thinking of my American friend Betty, who enjoys discussing her sexual experiences. "American men hate condoms. I have heard every excuse in the world," she says. Like most women, Betty has heard the many reasons why men are against wearing condoms.

The most common excuses are:

- Condoms will reduce my pleasure

- I'm allergic

- They don't fit

- I trust you, don't you trust me?

- I want to feel all of you

- You're the only one

When a sexual partner asks you to use condoms, don't guilt them by questioning their trust or love. It is about protection. I will not applaud those of you who play tricks to avoid using condoms. In October of 2021, California became the first state[17] to make the nonconsensual removal of a condom during sex (known as stealthing) a civil offense. Stealthing is assault and can land you in front of a judge.

According to the CDC (Center for Disease Control), in 2019, U.S. health departments reported:

- 1.8 million cases of chlamydia, an increase of nearly 20% since 2015

- 616,392 cases of gonorrhea, an increase of more than 50 % since 2015

- 129,813 cases of syphilis (all stages), an increase of more than 70% since 2015[18]

Risking an STD or an unwanted pregnancy is not a reasonable way to ask someone to demonstrate their love and trust. Chlamydia, HIV, HPV, and herpes can be present for years without noticeable symptoms. To recap, don't be a dick about condoms.

La capote c'est le soulier de verre de notre génération, on l'enfile quand on rencontre une inconnue, on danse toute la nuit, et puis on la balance…la capote je veux dire, pas l'inconnue."

—Marla Singer, *Fight Club*[19]

("The condom is the glass slipper of our generation, we put it on when we meet a stranger, we dance all night, and then we throw it away…the condom I mean, not the stranger.")

Sexless Relationships

Dear Guy,

My wife of five years has a high sex drive. I masturbate on occasion, but my libido is pretty nonexistent. Any advice?

- Ryan, 35

Dear Ryan,

Sorry to hear that you and your wife are not sexually on the same wavelength. You are only 35; you shouldn't give your wife the impression that she is married to a priest. We all have lethargic periods with libido. Low libido is not just a male problem. It happens to men and women alike.

If you are not having sex with your wife regularly, don't fool yourself into thinking that your relationship is fine. A relationship without sex and passion makes you roommates, not husband and wife. Regardless of her commitment to you, she is still human and has desires that should never go unsatisfied. There are always candidates for your succession.

I am not sure if your issue is a lack of libido, erectile dysfunction, or both. I recommend that you see your doctor to rule out any medical issues. Perhaps you are simply in a rut and need to spice things up to get you going again. Masturbate together, use toys, try something new. French women love surprises. Why not make suggestions to rendezvous at unusual locations and at different times? Use your imagination, you are young and not sexually dead yet. The desire for sex dulls with time for men and women. You are lucky that your partner is on fire. That is not always the case.

All the best,

Guy

Faire l'amour c'est le seul moyen de dépasser les différences qui isolent deux êtres.

—G. Blaise

("Making love is the only way to overcome the differences that isolate two beings.")

Imposters

Avoid being an imposter. If you do not like your current circumstances, do something to change them. Take a class, find a career, get a second job, put those earnings into savings, learn about investments, start your own company. Solitude is not a punishment. When you work on improving yourself, you will become a better partner to someone else.

Un homme sans argent est un loup sans dents.

—French proverb

("A man without money is a wolf without teeth.")

Divorcing Your Children

It is impossible to measure the suffering of children after their parents split. Yes, children are resilient, but that resiliency does not prevent them from heartache. I have been there. I know that the American justice system is not always kind to fathers and many of us have had to fight for our right to be in our children's lives.

It is deeply troubling to see some of you so willing to walk away from your children, even when no one is putting up a fight. The anger you may feel toward your ex should never be greater than the love you feel for your children. Some of you walk away and start brand new lives as if the children from your first marriage never existed. Inflicting that type of rejection onto a child is a clear demonstration of your character. Don't allow circumstances to keep you from being a good father to your children.

Divorces can get messy and downright vicious. True, there are some women who will use the children as pawns to hurt their spouse. This is why it is so important to be mindful of who you date and who you have sex with, even when you have no intention of making a baby. Without getting to know the character of your partner intimately, you may find yourself in a situation where you realize too late that you made a child with someone who will not place the child's best interest over causing you pain.

Un père n'est pas celui qui donne la vie.
Un père c'est celui qui participe activement à la vie de ses enfants.

—G. Blaise

("A father is not one who partners in the creation of life.
A father is one who actively participates in the lives of his children.")

Strong Women

Loving a strong woman requires confidence. If a strong woman allows you into her life, just know that you are wanted, not needed. A strong woman will get things done without you. Don't expect her to give you a "honey-do" list and then sit around waiting for you to complete the list. There are no distinctions between male and female responsibilities in her world. If you are adding to her joy and peace, she will appreciate you. If you are draining her resources and time, she will cut you loose.

If you play your cards right, the sex will be out of this world. In the bedroom is where you might have a chance in hell of getting a strong woman to relinquish control. There are few things as erotic as a strong woman completely and willingly giving in to passion and letting you take the lead.

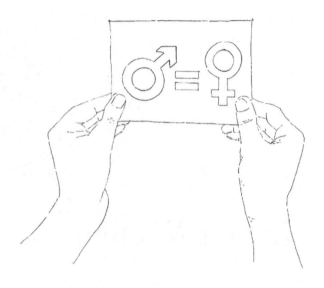

L'homme fort sera capable de gérer une femme forte, un homme faible dira qu'elle a un mauvais caractère.

—Laura Mistretta[20]

("A strong man will be able to handle a strong woman, a weak man will say that she has a bad character.")

Cocky Confidence

A good cock is not enough to make you a good lover, in the same way that owning a nice boat does not necessarily make you a skillful sailor. Many of you believe that your dick is your greatest asset and you rely on it to get by. My friend Kimberly, who dates men based on their dick size, tells me that men who are well endowed tend to be more arrogant and less kind in relationships. I am not suggesting that this is true for everyone, but this has been her experience. Don't let the overconfidence of having a big dick keep you from improving other qualities within yourself.

Le pénis est un instrument capricieux sur qui l'on ne peut guère compter, encombrant quand il ne sert à rien ... [et] partagent rarement les idées de son propriétaire ...

—Jean Dutourd[21]

("The penis is a finicky instrument that cannot be relied upon, cumbersome when of no use...and rarely shares the ideas of its owner...")

Hands-On Parenting

Dear Guy,

My girlfriend and I are expecting our first child. She often ac-
cuses me of not being invested enough in the pregnancy. Any advice on how to be a better partner and a good father in the future?

- Robert, IA

Dear Robert,

Congratulations on the new baby. It's important that both of you
give each other emotional support. You don't want to put yourself in
the position of sperm donor. We develop fatherly instincts in the same
way that a woman's motherly instincts kick in when the baby is born.

I have to admit that I had no idea what to expect with my first
child. I studied chemistry and biology all of my life, but when it came
to pregnancy, I had no clue what was going on in my partner's body.

I recall her asking me to put my hand on her belly to feel the baby moving. That sensation made fatherhood so real for me. Appearing invested in the pregnancy can be just a matter of attending those doctor's appointments with her and being more attentive to her as the due date approaches. Take on more of the household chores.

Be prepared for your lives to change completely. You will no longer be the center of your own universe. Your worlds will revolve around a tiny human who will only eat, poop, and cry for quite some time.

Here are a few suggestions to get you started on the right foot and build a natural symbiosis with your baby:

- Wake up at night for feedings, even if mom is breast-feeding.

- Tell your boss that you just became a father. Take time off from work.

- Learn to change diapers and bathe your baby.

- Thank the person who invented YouTube: you can learn how to hold and carry a baby—and anything else you want to learn about caring for your newborn.

- Don't worry too much and give yourself time. As long as you are a hands-on dad, your parenting skills will surely grow.

I do understand the pressure that you must be going through. Pregnancy can arouse anxiety in you as you get closer to the delivery date. It's not about being perfect, it's about being there.

Lastly, don't feel excluded or jealous of the newborn's relationship with mom. Understand that the baby will be her sole focus at the start. It's not necessarily true that a man who struggles during pregnancy will be a bad father. The fact that you are concerned enough to ask for advice tells me that you will be a great dad.

Best of luck,

Guy

La parentalité, c'est comme la chimie, il faut deux corps pour avoir une réaction.

—G. Blaise

("Parenthood is like chemistry, it takes two bodies to have a reaction.")

Suggestion Box

When she makes suggestions during lovemaking, she is not calling you a bad lover—don't be offended—she is trying to make the moment more pleasurable for herself. Sometimes you must put your ego aside and listen to her. Ask questions if you are unsure. I consider all feedback in bed as positive. Some will be compliments and some will improve my odds of earning more compliments. At the end of the day, her feedback can only make you a better lover.

Un couple n'est vraiment qu'un couple que s'il transpire.
—Frédéric Dard[22]
("A couple is only a couple if they sweat.")

In the Closet

Alex, a 26-year-old man who I knew as straight—he had a girl-friend when we were in college—today is openly gay. He tells me, "While I recognize the progress made by society in accepting us as who we are, that same society forces us to stay in the closet. We often hide to avoid the pressure and expectations of our families. My parents' religious beliefs were the reason it took three years for them to accept me as their son—their gay son. Religion tends to focus on sexuality while other acts mentioned in the Bible are routinely overlooked."

Marrying a woman to hide your sexuality is a dangerous game without winners. Some of these marriages result in children, which often causes a great deal of pain when the truth boils to the surface—as it inevitably does. I am not referring to a *mariage blanc* (white marriage) where both parties willingly agree to enter a marriage of convenience. I am referring to the men whose wives have no idea that their husbands have sexual involvements with other men. This behavior places their wives at risk without their knowledge or consent. I do not pretend to be able to understand your reasoning or shame or pain, but I imagine the weight of such a lie must be difficult on your shoulders.

*Quand le mensonge prend l'ascenseur, la verité l'escalier,
elle met plus de temps mais elle finit toujours par arriver."*

—G. Blaise

("When the lie takes the elevator, the truth takes the stairs.
It takes longer but it always gets there.")

Your GPS Won't Help

The number of American men who are unable to correctly label a diagram of a vagina is embarrassingly high. Likewise, the number of unsatisfied wives is also unfortunately high. It is time to put your pride aside and learn how to pleasure a woman. According to a 2017 article in the *New York Post*, a survey conducted by The Eve Appeal for Gynecological Cancer Awareness Month asked 1,000 men to label the vagina on a diagram of a vagina, vulva, cervix, ovaries, and the fallopian tubes. Only 500 correctly labeled the vagina.[23]

According to a 2015 U.S. probability survey, 81% of the 1,055 respondents reported not being able to orgasm through vaginal penetration alone.[24] So, it is important to know a woman's anatomy and other ways to bring her pleasure. There are over 8,000 nerve endings on the clitoris,[25] so do not make the mistake of ignoring it. Penetrating too soon is like taking a shortcut on a recipe. Rushing into penetration can be painful for her. When you are truly giving her pleasure, she will not be in a hurry to make you come. Do your homework, invest some time in acquiring more knowledge on this topic, read, and don't be shy about asking her what she likes.

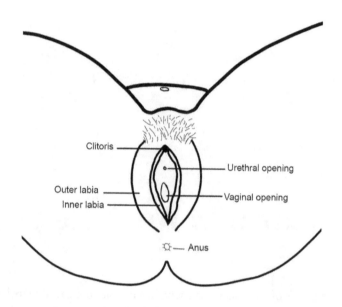

Une femme heureuse au lit est une femme fidèle.

—French saying

("A woman happy in bed is a faithful woman.")

Body Shaming

Being in a relationship does not give us a pass to body shame. Some of you consider your body shaming to be harmless jokes, while some of you are trying to manipulate and control with your intentional comments. Women are subjected to false and unattainable beauty standards from the time they are children. Television, movies, magazines, social media, all contribute to insecurities about weight, breast size, hair, complexion, the list goes on.

Body shaming can lead to eating disorders, depression, risky surgeries, and worse. A study by NOW (National Organization for Women), reports that at age 13, 53% of American girls are unhappy with their bodies. This grows to 78% by the time girls reach 17, and by age 60, 28.7% of women feel dissatisfied with their bodies.[26]

I don't know many people who are the same size they were in high school. We all change over time. Many women we know have brought life into this world. Those of us—men—lacking ovaries and the levels of estrogen that women produce have no business commenting on the changes they can cause. Unless she's actively asking for your opinion, keep your mouth shut. If she asks for help, be supportive. Try making healthy meals together. Pick up a sport that you will both enjoy and schedule a block of time each day to exercise together.

If you are fond of breasts with huge implants, then marry someone who has them. Don't try to talk your partner into risky surgery just so you can play with the melons of your pornographic dreams. I doubt she is shaming you for the inadequacy that is your cock (unless you're into that). Some of you are bad-mouthing your wives to your friends and co-workers. Don't be that guy.

Choose a partner for her inner qualities, her intellect, her humor, the way she sees the world, and you will be off to a great relationship. When someone exudes positivity and confidence, it makes them attractive inside and out. Stop being shallow and only looking at the outward appearance. I understand that we all have preferences. I am not suggesting you suppress chasing after the qualities you find attractive. I am saying that you should devote some time into finding out a woman's inner qualities as well. Are you intellectually compatible? Do you have similar views and goals? There is much more that goes into a healthy relationship than just being physically attracted to each other.

Your words matter. Be more aware of your criticism, or so-called jokes. When you love someone, your words should be uplifting and supportive. With so many daily opportunities for a woman to be exposed to body shaming, her partner should provide the one safe space where she is loved as she is—unconditionally.

N'ouvre la bouche que si tu es sûr que ce que tu vas dire est plus beau que le silence.

—French saying

("Only open your mouth if you're sure what you're going to say is more beautiful than silence.")

Dating Women with Children

Dating a woman with children requires an extra level of flexibility and understanding on your part. Be honest about your intentions. She may only introduce you to the kids if she thinks the relationship is going somewhere. With that in mind, be sure that you are open to 'going somewhere' before agreeing to meet them.

You will have to be okay with not being the top priority. She may be in communication with the children's father and you will have to be okay with that as well. There is a difference between visiting a woman with children and spending a few nights at her place and physically moving in. Unless she asks, do not involve yourself in the discipline—this is a surefire way to cause conflict in the relationship. Always remember, she is a mother first before she is your lover.

L'amour d'une mère pour son enfant ne connait ni loi, ni pitié,
ni limite.
Il pourrait aneantir impitoyablement tout ce qui se trouve en travers
de son chemin.

—Agatha Christie[27]

("A mother's love for her child knows no law, no pity, no limit.
She could ruthlessly destroy anything that stands in her way.")

Couch Potato

Many couples enjoy watching television together. Curled up on the couch with a good movie or series can be a great way to unwind after a long day at work. On the other hand, too much television by one partner can kill the communication and cause resentment. Watching game after game while your wife is doing the housework is not going to make her feel appreciated.

Taking on the role of a piece of furniture in the house does not nurture a healthy relationship. I am not suggesting you deprive yourself of watching your favorite team now and then. I am saying that sitting in front of the television should not be the only thing you do the moment you step through the door. Everything in moderation, including social media.

"Si le vœux des maris paresseux était exaucé,
il n'y aurait aucune sortie des poubelles."

—G. Blaise

"If the wish of lazy husbands were granted,
there would be no taking out the trash."

Meeting Her Family

Many of you have already had this experience. It is time for you to show her family that you are worthy of her company. In the French culture, we bring a gift when meeting her family for the first time. A bottle of wine is a good option. In general, American men dress quite casually; some of you make no effort at all. There is a French saying, "We recognize the monk by his clothes." You will be judged by your words, actions, and appearance, so dress to impress.

Public displays of affection are as common in France as Eiffel Tower souvenirs in Paris. Do not be afraid to display tasteful gestures of affection, such as holding her hand. Of course, I am not suggesting you hump her leg at the dinner table. Use your discretion. Be observant of your surroundings and comment on something unique you may notice. Compliment the food and the chef. Offer to help clean up before leaving the table. Lastly, don't talk for the sake of talking. The ability to be a good listener is a valuable quality. It is not necessary for her family to approve of you, but it makes life easier when they do.

"Qui veut aller loin ménage son attitude."

—G. Blaise

("He who wants to go far spares his attitude.")

Romance Takes Effort

It is no coincidence that movies centered around love and romance are a favorite among women. Girl meets boy, they fall in love and live happily ever after. It isn't easy to compete with the heroes in the movies that do and say everything right. It can leave men falling short of their partner's expectations. Living up to a Hallmark movie is impossible.

I am not suggesting that you have to say "I love you" every hour or buy gifts for your partner each day. As men, we are not always ready and available to provide affection or to be thoughtful when needed. We can be insensitive at times. We are all different, some of us are naturally more romantic than others. Being romantic can be a learned skill. With minimal effort, you can learn ways to be more in tune with your partner's need for romance.

Here are some romantic suggestions that your partner might enjoy:

- Plan a picnic somewhere with a view.

- Select a meaningful puzzle to build together.

- Hold hands more.

- Take walks together.

- Take a culinary or art class together.

- Plan a weekend getaway.

- Work on a DIY project together.

Even when you are at a loss for the right words, the important thing is that you demonstrate proof of love every day. Concrete acts can say more than words.

Quand nous perdons la romance, il y a des problèmes a venir.

—G. Blaise

("When we lose romance, there is trouble ahead.")

Male G-Spot

Straight men have no problem being on the giving end of anal sex with their wives or girlfriends, but the idea of receiving pleasure through ass play often evokes a negative reaction. Enjoying anal stimulation by a woman does not make you gay. Don't let your low-key homophobia keep you from experiencing immense pleasure. Putting psychological barriers on your sexuality limits your pleasure.

Your prostate is the equivalent of the female G-spot. It is referred to as the P-spot and is surrounded by thousands of nerve endings. Stimulation of the prostate gland can cause a mind-blowing orgasm.

If she trusts you to slide your entire dick into her ass, you can certainly trust her to reciprocate with a finger. Some straight men have discovered the pleasure of ass stimulation and are enjoying more than her fingers. All it takes is trust, communication, an open mind, and plenty of lube.

S'ouvrir à la réciprocité, c'est se libérer pour toujours de la prison de soi-même. "

—Roland Poupon[28]

("To open up to reciprocity is to free oneself forever from the prison of oneself.")

Being Funny Is Not Enough

Humor is one of the qualities that I find appealing about American women. French women tend to be more reserved when it comes to making jokes and laughing, while American women do not hold back in that regard. Laughing together as a couple is bonding and healthy.

If you ask American women what they look for in a man, a good sense of humor is near the top of the list, if not first. But, be aware that being funny alone doesn't make you a great provider. If being funny was enough to make a woman happy, single comedians would not exist. It takes love, affection, and financial stability to maintain a happy home.

When you first met your partner, were you being witty and funny to make her laugh? After years of marriage, are you still doing the same, or are you only sharing your humor with friends and co-workers? If your wit and humor are part of what attracted her to you, then keep that going. Remind her now and then of why she fell in love with you in the first place. A great sense of humor is just one of many things that make a man a great catch.

Un homme doit prendre soin de sa femme, et une femme doit prendre soin de son homme. Aucun n'est plus important que l'autre. Les plus belles relations se construisent à deux.

—Lesmotspositifs.com

("A man should take care of his wife, and a wife should take care of her husband. Neither is more important than the other. The best relationships are built together.")

Gaslighting

Gaslighting is emotional abuse and manipulation. It is a cowardly way to gain control. If you do any of the following, you are gaslighting your partner:

- You make your partner question how she feels about your inappropriate behavior.

- You dismiss her communication by saying she is overreacting.

- You tell her that she is not recalling the events of an incident correctly.

Gaslighting creates a toxic relationship. If you recognize yourself engaging in these behaviors, it is time for you to seek professional treatment.

Le pervers narcissique accompli se montre socialisé, séducteur, socialement conforme et se voulant supernormal: la normalité, c'est son meilleur déguisement.

—Paul-Claude Racamier[29]

("The accomplished narcissistic pervert shows himself to be socialized, seductive, socially compliant, and wanting to be supernormal: normalcy is his best disguise.")

Avoiding Your Home

Those of you working to support your family have an obliga-
tion to find a good balance between work and home life.   I
have heard many absent husbands say, "I don't have a choice."
Indeed, it is a choice that you are making to never be at home.
Often times, your wives are also working while taking care of the
children and the house.

I hear many American women complaining about your discon-
nect with reality. You seem to always believe that everything is fine
as long as your partner and children are sheltered. Intentionally or
unintentionally, you don't want to see or listen when your partner
is physically and mentally exhausted.

I am not blaming you for working. Better a man who has a job
and is absent than a man who is present but contributes nothing. Sometimes a woman wants your physical presence to give her
emotional support—your arms around her are priceless. There is
no chance for a couple to survive if they love each other but hardly
spend time together.

It is also true that some of you are physically present, but emotionally elsewhere. It is no different than being out of the house. This behavior can cause loneliness, even when you are both in the same room. Again, it is your choice. Lost time can never be made up.

Un homme qui évite sa maison, laisse derrière lui un lit froid et un partenaire solitaire.

—G. Blaise

("A man who avoids his home, leaves behind a cold bed and a lonely partner.")

Independent Women

I notice many of you do not appreciate an independent woman, one who does not rely on a partner to meet her needs. Some women were raised to be independent; others learned to become independent after a life experience. A woman's feelings for you should never be in question. If she makes time for you, that should tell you all you need to know. Be sure to add to her quality of life, not diminish it. You have to be confident of your place in her world. Give her some space to make her own decisions and to be herself.

Une femme indépendante économiquement peut se réaliser dans des tas de domaines, y compris en amour.

—Gisele Halimi[30]

("An economically independent woman can fulfill herself in many areas, including love.")

Religion

Far too many of you who profess to be Christians are doing un-Christian-like things. Women who seek men on Christian dating sites are hoping to find commonality in a partner who is God-fearing. Instead, they are encountering predators, users, liars, and cheaters who are using scripture as an excuse to control and abuse women. Don't be that guy. Pretending to be something you are not will never end well. If religion is important to her, be honest with yourself and with her. If religion is not a big part of your life, then stay off the Christian dating apps.

L'homme de Dieu est un parfait hypocrite.
Même le prêtre a onze érections par jour.

—*G. Blaise*

("The man of God is a perfect hypocrite.
Even the priest has eleven erections a day.")

Relationships Are Doomed without Respect

For those of you in long-term relationships, this chapter is for you. Lack of respect is a common complaint among women I have interviewed. They also say that their men put on a very different persona when interacting with people outside of the relationship. Most of their family and friends are not aware of their behavior within the relationship.

What makes you such a petulant killjoy? The daily negativity makes your home unpleasant and your wife unhappy (not to mention the children). Don't be surprised if she one day decides that she's had enough and moves on. If you are unhappy with yourself, it is never too late to make some changes. If you are unhappy with your wife, communicate; make an attempt to improve the relationship. Sometimes, there is no repairing a relationship and the best thing for both of you is to end it—a far better solution than suffering needlessly in an unhealthy and toxic union.

Quand la colère emplit ton cœur, ne laisse pas ta langue aboyeren vain.

—Sappho[31]

("When anger fills your heart, do not let your tongue bark in vain.")

The Orchestra of Lovemaking Has Many Instruments

A couple that can maintain love and desire for each other has the upper hand. Men often think that sex is the key to happiness. For us, sex is a physical need at a specific moment. Sex certainly contributes to happiness, but it is not everything. Affection and acts of love are equally important. Here are some ideas on thoughtful acts of love:

WRITTEN WORDS ARE POWERFUL

One of my habits before sex is to use the power of my words. I find that texting during the day is a very effective way to send a signal to my partner that she is wanted. Stimulating the mind is the perfect appetizer to a five-course meal. A carefully-written text will build up excitement until you can be face to face.

HOSTING YOUR LOVER AT YOUR PLACE

Take the time to be prepared. Clean sheets, towels, and an organized place will make her feel comfortable. She will surely notice and appreciate your effort. Have her favorite drink, music, and snacks on hand. You don't have to spend a fortune to be thoughtful and romantic.

SEX IS NOT ALWAYS ON THE TABLE

Sex is not the only way to show love and desire. If your partner is not in the mood, don't take that as a sign to disappear into another room. Offer her a massage, no strings attached. Maybe she would prefer a foot rub. Massages can provide a good time to bond with conversation and physical touch.

WHEN SEX IS ON THE TABLE

Again, be prepared. Have oils, lubrication, and condoms ready. Unless you are in a monogamous relationship and have discussed the topic carefully, always use protection. STDs and unplanned pregnancies can be easily avoided with a bit of responsibility. *The Kama Sutra* was my favorite book of sexual positions in my younger days. Don't be afraid to try something new.

AN ABUNDANCE OF KISSES

Going straight for the breasts and vagina is a rookie move. Kiss her shoulders, caress her back and hair, kiss her neck, legs, and inner thighs. Don't be in a hurry to get to the end. I can't stress this enough.

Every woman is unique and not all will enjoy my suggestions. You have to invest the time to get to know your partner and learn her likes and dislikes. Don't feel shy about asking direct questions and give her time to connect with you. Just as guys need sex to open up to love, women need love to open up to sex.

Un ouvrier qui veut bien faire le travail doit d'abord préparer ses outils.

—G. Blaise

("A worker who wants to do his job well must first prepare his tools.")

Fathers of Daughters

I applaud many of you who are the fathers of daughters who changed your vision about women after you became a dad. Young daughters of today are the future wives of tomorrow. If you are one of those fathers who have daughters but do not respect women, it is an attitude to revise.

I do believe that if you are a father of daughters you have to be a feminist. If feminism offends you, you misunderstand its meaning. Being a feminist means that you support equal rights for all genders. Confident men have no problem being feminists because they know it takes nothing away from them to support women's pursuit of equality. I think it's important that men change their patriarchal attitudes in the twenty-first century.

Encourage your daughters to be outspoken, to say "NO" when necessary, and to pursue any career and life path they wish. A good father will want his daughters to pursue their dreams without the worry of gender roles or traditions.

Tout homme porte en soi une image de la femme
qui lui vient de sa mere:
c'est elle qui le détermine a respecter les femmes ...

—Friedrich Wilhelm Nietzsche[32]

("Every man carries within himself an image of women which
comes to him from his mother.
It is she who determines his respect for women.")

Porn King

Congratulations! All that porn you've watched will make you the lover of the century. Just kidding. All the banging and awkward positions you learned from pornography is irrelevant and will make you a lousy lover. Porn can become a distraction from finding a partner or interacting with a current partner.

A study done by the Institute for the Study of Labor suggests that men who view pornography are less likely to be married than men who do not.[33] Michael Malcolm, an associate professor of economics at West Chester University of Pennsylvania who co-authored the research said, "We think that the study makes a convincing argument. Pornography increases the alternatives for sexual gratification."[34]

Learn to explore a woman's body. Let your dick take a back seat to your mouth and fingers. Penetration should not happen only once during sex. Enter her and then pull out. Don't let yourself go. This will take self-control and practice. Go back to exploring her body some more. Only when she is visibly worn out should you allow yourself to finish.

Le sexe c'est comme l'orthographe: Plus tu pratiques et moins tu fais d'erreurs.

—French saying

("Sex is like spelling, the more you practice, the fewer mistakes you make.")

Living with Your Parents

Things can happen in life especially during an economic crisis, maybe you need to transition careers or you are moving in with your parents to save money to start a business or to go to school. That is acceptable. But I want to talk about some of you who have adopted the attitude of a parasite: those who move in and wait until your parents die to inherit their wealth. Many of you don't even contribute to the household and have no problem letting Mom do your laundry. I am not sure how you expect to start a family when you are grown adult men without a place of your own. Whether or not you are saving money, it appears irresponsible and immature to potential partners.

La maturité c'est quand on quitte ses parents pour devenir parent aussi.

—Thomas Gatabazi[35]

("Maturity is when you leave your parents to become a parent too.")

You're Not Smarter than a Woman

Women are born with intuition and are attentive to the slightest changes. Unfortunately for us, we have limited intuition or have no inkling on how to tap into that sense. No matter who you are, rich or poor, remember this—do not lie to a woman.

Women are natural born lie detectors. They can sense every suspicious activity of yours and if they want to investigate, they will discover the truth. It does not matter if you cover your tracks and leave no trace of your lies, she will know that you are lying, even if she doesn't know what you are lying about. The worst thing that you can do to yourself is to undermine and underestimate a woman's capacity to know when you are being dishonest.

L'intuition féminine est meilleure que n'importe quel détective privé.

—French saying

("Female intuition is better than any private investigator.")

Baby Mama Drama

For many of you, making children with many women is a sport. The pleasure of sex is so intense that you forget that a child brought into this world needs love and care. Some of you intentionally refuse to pay child support or spend time with your children. If you are doing things intentionally to punish your ex, you are punishing your children. They are the victims of your irresponsibility. If you choose to ghost your kids, sooner or later, there is a price to pay for that.

Consider having a vasectomy if you insist on not using condoms. It will prevent you from making babies that you can't or won't support, and it is completely reversible.

Un coureur de jupons n'est fidèle qu'à sa réputation.

—G. Blaise

("A womanizer is only faithful to his reputation.")

Communication

Perfection doesn't exist in a relationship. If you find yourself being accused of not communicating and you know in your heart that you want this relationship to work, here are a few things you can do:

Start your evening by asking her about her day. Ask her opinion about something in the news to start a conversation.

Try listening closely and engaging more. I think when we meet someone, we are distracted by the beauty or the intellect, and communication is not always a quality that many of us look for at the start of a relationship.

Lack of communication seems to be a French couple's obsession and I realize that American couples face the same challenges. If you are dating right now, it's important to think about how you solve your differences. This can give you an idea of what your relationship will be like in the long term. Women, too, can be noncommunicative. I think a couple who finds an effective way to communicate avoids a breakup. So many people in relationships lock themselves in silence.

As a parent today, I would never tell my child "Go cry in your room." I see that as another way of suppressing feelings.

If you are in a relationship with a noncommunicative person, make an effort to learn to communicate and consider counseling. A lack of communication will doom a relationship sooner or later.

Les maris sont les meilleurs personnes avec qui partager des secrets. Ils ne diront jamais rien a personne, parce qu'en réalité, ils ne t'ont pas écouté.

—G. Blaise

("Husbands are the best people to share secrets with. They will never say anything to anyone, because in reality, they did not listen to you.")

Climaxing

Many of you have been in long-term relationships but still wonder why your partner doesn't climax. Since many of you are notoriously selfish when it comes to pleasing your women in bed, I realize that the best way to make love to your lover is to take an anatomy course and read a lot of women's magazines. Throughout my interviews with women, the majority of them say that you come up short in bed. The game is over once you orgasm or you cannot keep up your erection, leaving her frustrated.

According to board-certified obstetrician and gynecologist Dr. Tatnai Burnett from the Mayo Clinic, most women are orgasmic only during stimulation of the clitoris.[36] Very few women experience orgasms during vaginal penetration. With this in mind, place your attention where it is needed most and remember to take your time.

If you refuse to make changes, you can't be surprised when she turns you down. She is bored, especially when it becomes a chore. For many of you who believe in only banging the pussy, you are missing the target. Many women figure it is best to simulate an orgasm to make you think that you are great. To enjoy lovemaking, it is important that you know your partner's body and your own body. You should ask your partner what turns her on and communicate.

Le sexe, c'est comme la cuisine.
Tout le monde peut le faire, mais tout le monde n'est pas chef.

—G. Blaise

("Sex is like cooking. Anyone can do it, but not everyone is a chef.")

Generosity

You don't have to be rich to be generous. Generosity comes from the heart. Small gestures of appreciation and admiration should be a regular occurrence when you are in a relationship.

One major cultural difference between America and France is that French men don't ask women to split the bill on a date. I have heard American women say they prefer it when men do not pay the bill because then they feel no pressure to have sex afterward. If you expect a woman to have sex with you because you bought her a meal, you must re-evaluate your definition of a man. If a woman agrees to make time to meet you in person, to get to know you over dinner, she owes you absolutely nothing. If you are struggling financially and can't afford to treat her, be honest about your situation from the start. This is not something that a date wants to discover at the dinner table.

La generosité n'est ni inculquée en famille ni apprisé a l'église. La generosité est innée.

—Thomas Gatabazi[37]

("Generosity is neither inculcated in family nor learned in church. Generosity is innate.")

Online Dating Dos
and Don'ts

Online dating is a multibillion-dollar industry. In a study done by Michael Rosenfeld in 2019, a sociologist from Stanford University, meeting online has become the most popular way for Americans to find a partner.[38]

Jasmine, 27, talks openly about her online dating experiences. She said, "You have to sift through the many men on dating apps pretending to want a serious relationship. I'm sure the reason they are not honest about their intentions is because most women on dating apps are looking for a commitment, not just a hook up."[39]

Emma, 31, says, "I have been ghosted a few times by men I met online. It would be nice if they were honest about how they feel after a date. Is it so hard to tell someone that you do not feel a connection with them? I would rather hear him say that than to disappear. It's immature and cowardly. Still, online dating is better than the alternative. I don't like bars or big crowds, so either I meet men online or don't meet them at all. The grocery store has never worked for me."[40]

Steven, 29, said, "I've gone out with a few women in person that I met on dating sites. They start off great and then they are quick to act like a girlfriend before we even get to that level. Sometimes they get too comfortable too fast and are soon asking me to buy them things. I move on when that happens."[41]

Online dating takes persistence and a thick skin. If you have both, the law of averages will do its thing and you will eventually find someone worthy of your time.

1. Check your spelling and grammar. Learn the difference between your and you're.

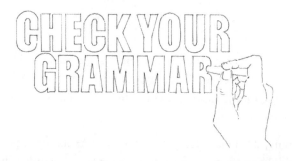

2. Read women's profiles. Many of you are ignoring the profiles and communicating solely based on her pictures. If her profile says that smoking is a dealbreaker, don't waste her time if you are a smoker.

3. "Ask me anything." This comment is no better than a blank profile. Make an effort to share a few thoughts that reflect you best. This appears lazy and is a huge turn-off.

4. If she is looking for someone local, respect that. Long distance relationships come with their own set of challenges.

5. Posting pictures of your children on the internet is not appealing to women. If you think this will get you a woman who loves children, it is a miscalculation. Write about how important your children are to you and leave out the pictures—there are too many creeps on the internet, not to mention the fact that your ex-spouse would probably not appreciate learning there are pictures of her children on dating apps.

6. "I have big feet." No, there is no connection between big feet and a big dick. Change your strategy.

is There Any Truth to
Shoe Size = Penis Size?

7. There was a time when having differences in politics was not a big deal. Today, Americans are so divided in their beliefs that sharing your perspective up front may help you make more compatible matches from the start.

8. "Let's order pizza at my place and watch a movie." Don't invite a woman over to your place to meet for the first time. One out of every six American women have been victims of rape or attempted rape.[42] It is completely insensitive to push this suggestion without giving her time to get to know you. Give her time to feel safe about visiting you at home. It should always be her call. Any public setting such as a local café or bar is a better choice than inviting her over.

9. Military service men and pilots are always on the move. Don't use your career, whether real or made up, to pull hit and runs. Many of you on dating sites have no desire to be in a relationship. If you only want sex, then say so. The karma from playing with women's emotions will be tenfold.

10. Your blurry pictures immediately scream, "I am cheating!" If you are not sneaking around, share clear pictures of yourself and take off the sunglasses.

11. "I am married to my roommate." Does your roommate know this?

12. "I love God, use drugs, and drink often." Don't bother pursuing a woman with extreme differences.

13. Do not take pictures in bed. A woman once said to me, "If I see a headboard in his pictures, I keep moving."

14. Keep your clothes on for your profile pictures. She can see your muscles under a fitted shirt.

15. Stop posting pictures of your fancy toys instead of yourself.

16. Don't say, "I love to work out in my spare time" if you don't mean it or enjoy it. The body doesn't lie.

17. If you are seeking older women, be honest about your intentions. Are you in search of a mother figure or someone who will take care of you? If you are not willing to have a long-term relationship with an older woman, tell her what you want.

18. Avoid dating sites while you are going through a divorce, unless it is amicable and free of drama. Being "separated" is

a red flag for single women. It implies that your life is messy and you are not ready to move on.

19. Create profile names that don't make you seem like an immature teenager. Women don't find this attractive. "MrHotDick69" "ErectileReptile10" "BigOne50"

20. "This picture was taken one month ago." Avoid embarrassing yourself if you show up 25 pounds heavier and older. It's unlikely you gained 25 pounds and went bald in four weeks.

21. If you are ghosting women who are not ready to jump into bed with you, they have dodged a bullet.

Just the Tips

1. Attraction to a woman starts by the way you present yourself. Hygiene is important. Showers, grooming, and a splash of cologne will go a long way. Dress for the occasion. A few nice outfits won't kill you.

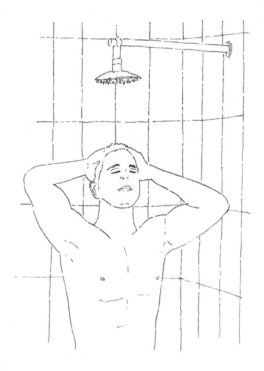

2. There is a difference between confidence and aggressiveness. Aggressive men are not sexy. A woman will judge the way you behave around others.

3. The key to keeping your lover satisfied is to make her vibrate from head to toe. Learn about a woman's body and how it works. Don't just fuck if you are not capable of giving your partner quality. Quality means time and intimacy.

4. Don't be in a hurry to penetrate and finish in five pumps. Get better at satisfying her sexual needs or she will find someone who can, and that will be on you.

5. Your phone is a big distraction. Turn it off and give her your undivided attention.

6. A healthy diet, along with regular exercise, will help maintain stamina in bed. You can't expect to perform your best when you are fueling yourself with garbage. The typical American diet is loaded with processed foods and sugar. Be mindful of what you consume and your body will reward you with better sex. You will become more attractive to her and your semen will taste better, too.

7. A modern man understands the importance of sharing household tasks if he is living with a partner. Do not wait to be asked for a hand with something like doing the dishes, doing laundry, making the bed, and setting the table. Pick up your underwear and socks. They won't jump in the laundry basket by themselves. Those are huge things that prevent conflicts in a relationship.

8. Not all dicks were created equal. Penises come in all sizes. At the end of the day, it's all about how you use it. If you are small, master oral sex and use toys with your partner. If you are big, don't let your ego surpass your skill, you still have to put in effort. A big dick doesn't guarantee satisfaction.

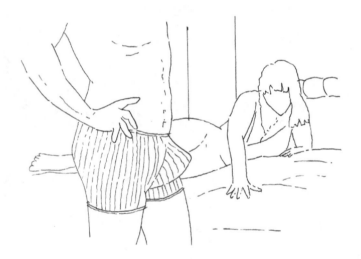

9. Honesty is the best policy when in a relationship. Women masturbate just like men for the same reason, it feels good. Never be shy about explaining to her that it's not about her. It is something to discuss with your partner. Discussion doesn't mean permission. It is not cheating. With that said, you will want to re-evaluate if your alone time is affecting the intimacy within the relationship.

10. Give her a culinary orgasm. A man who cooks for his partner is a golden man. Indeed, many women find it sexy. If you don't know how to cook, learn. Find out what dishes she likes and learn to make them. A culinary orgasm is as important as the one you can have in bed.

A simple recipe for the morning after a night of romance:

French Omelette

Ingredients

4 eggs

Salt (to taste)

Pepper (to taste)

1 tablespoon olive oil

½ cup grated cheese

Bread

Butter

Directions:

Crack eggs into a mixing bowl, being careful not to leave shells. Whisk thoroughly with the salt and pepper. Add olive oil to bottom of pan on medium to high heat. Pour eggs into pan and cook until bottom is golden, then flip the omelette. Add cheese on top while the other side cooks. Serve with toasted bread and butter and a seasoned green salad.

11. Eroticism starts with your hands. Giving a massage to your partner is a gift. Some men are fine paying for their partner to get a massage. If you are capable of doing so, she will appreciate you.

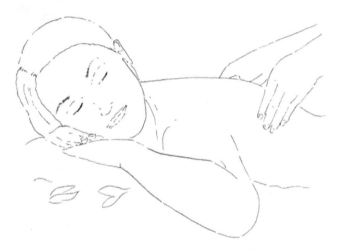

12. A way to show her love is to clean her car and fill up her gas tank while she is resting after a long week.

13. Real men don't play games. Nothing is more disrespectful than telling a woman what she wants to hear so that you can continue to sleep with her, knowing that you are not in love.

14. Be a nice guy. Contrary to popular belief, being nice does not mean you will finish last. I think many women who choose "bad boys" are actually choosing narcissists and end up regretting it in the long run. There are many women out there who appreciate kindness. Intelligent women do not confuse kindness with weakness.

15. Don't wait for Valentine's Day. Bring her flowers from time to time.

16. You don't have to be French to kiss right. French relationship expert Jacques Salome says, "A single kiss can awaken more emotion and pleasure than a long declaration of love."[43] Practice on your fingers, if necessary. When your lips meet, your lover will open her mouth while tilting her head, you do the same. Then your tongues meet and caress each other. It can last forever. Voila! Women complain that you are shoving your entire tongue in their mouths right from the start. The tongue should be involved progressively as the passion intensifies.

17. Use your tongue to explore your lover's body and alternate between licks and kisses.

18. Make a habit of kissing and licking your lover's body gently and softly, exploring her from head to toe.

19. Read women's magazines! You can learn a lot about what women want. It's like being a fly on the wall of a club for women only.

20. Use eye contact for intimacy. Women want us to be more expressive in bed and nothing is more expressive than a gaze during lovemaking. Eye to eye contact is like adding fuel to the fire. Through it, we can say everything because it is a language. Despite the stigmas of having sex in the missionary position, it is the best way to make eye contact during sex. The missionary position is chic and intimate, simple and sensual.

21. Dates to remember: her birthday, Mother's Day, Valentine's Day, and your wedding anniversary. Women may not be vocal about those dates, but you must anticipate and show your appreciation on those dates. You don't have to spend a lot of money. A romantic dinner can be had right at home. A meaningful gift will certainly be appreciated.

22. Show interest and support in what she does. The capacity to listen without interrupting your partner is a skill. Showing interest in what she does, her work, and her goals are signs that you are interested in who she is as a person. Above all, give her space to nurture her friendships without you. Being in a relationship shouldn't mean the end of other friendships, for either of you.

23. Women crave affection, they like to feel like they exist and that their opinion counts in relationships. Never make the mistake of saying that you have the final say.

24. The best way to receive love is to not stay in your shell but to open your heart.

25. Love is an antidepressant.

26. Never make your home a prison; your mate will eventually suffocate. Life at home needs to be agreeable.

27. People who are married for a long time are not perfect couples. They fight too. A couple that lasts is never a couple without challenges, but a couple who knows how to solve their differences.

28. Sometimes the reason partners seek a lover is not sexual dissatisfaction, but the lack of tenderness in their relationship.

29. The purpose of being a couple is to grow by facing all the obstacles together. Don't give up too quickly.

30. Your partner should not be a copy of you—embrace your differences. Differences can make it interesting.

31. Educate yourself, be aware of current affairs. Intelligence is a big turn-on for women.

32. Successful men can get just about any woman they want. Married or single, do whatever it takes to be financially stable. Many women are hypergamous.

33. If you are seeing someone, no matter how smart and handsome you think you are, never stop working on yourself or your relationship. Overconfidence has ruined many relationships.

34. If you meet a woman who is emotionally broken, know that it is not your job to fix her. You certainly can be supportive while she is working on herself.

35. Watching porn with your partner may seem exciting, but make sure she finds it exciting as well. Most women I have met do not like watching another woman being fucked. Words are important to turn a woman on and create a desire. I say this often, but it bears repeating. Sex does not begin in the bedroom. It begins with stimulation of her mind.

36. Don't waste your time lying to women, because they always know. It's not about evidence you leave or don't leave behind—it's a feeling women can sense. Women are intuitive at a level that men are unable to comprehend.

37. You can only run shit when she lets you run shit. Even submissive women have the ability to make you think you are in charge because she knows it is important to you. In truth, she is the mastermind behind all of your best ideas. There is nothing to be done about this. Just accept it and go with the flow, enjoying the rewards of her brilliance.

38. Making love to your partner regularly is as important as taking showers. Skipping showers, much like skipping sex, will make you single again.

39. Never order/urge/shame a woman to exercise. That's the job of her doctor. Let her take her own initiative and be there for support. Words of encouragement will always be appreciated.

40. Control your cock, never hit on or sleep with your ex's friends or family members. They are off limits.

41. Being handsome doesn't make you an asset. You will need to bring something else to the table.

42. A threesome is a fantasy for most men. Never bring it up to your partner unless she brings it up first. It is a big turn-off for most of women. Sometimes, a fantasy should remain a fantasy. If she is open to the idea, don't get ready. Men seem to always find a way to fuck up a good thing.

43. Learn to speak a foreign language. Men who speak more than one language are often opened-minded, thereby enriching their life and expanding their knowledge. According to a CNN article from 2017, "Does Being Bilingual Make You Sexy?" 71% of Americans and 61% of Britons believe speaking more than one language makes a person seem more attractive.[44] Knowing a second language can also be beneficial to your career.

44. Humor is good for the soul. You don't have to be Chris Rock to make her smile. We say in French, "A woman who laughs is halfway into your bed."

45. Sex is not a race. If she glances at the clock, you are doing it wrong.

46. Don't compare your dick to the ones you see in locker rooms. Focus on why you are there. Exercise is good for your overall well-being. A small penis can have power when combined with extended oral play and stamina.

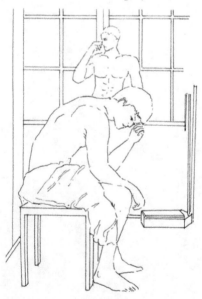

47. Notice her new hairstyle or outfit. She will appreciate your attention to the details.

48. Don't act like a child at the mention of tampons. Learn about her reproductive system and be helpful when it is her time of the month.

49. Don't ignore her messages. She knows you are never far from your phone.

50. Groom yourself! There is no reason for you to smell bad or look unkept. Even beards need grooming. It is a huge turn-off for women.

Relationships are complex and no two are the same. I believe that happiness can be achieved when both partners are committed to making the relationship work. No matter the circumstances, it is not your responsibility to make your partner happy. You can only facilitate her happiness by giving her your support when it is needed. The best way to be a good partner is to go into a relationship with your feet on the ground and your eyes wide open. In French it's called "realistic love." The magic words are compromise and communication.

We live in a period of emotional revolution, women define and redefine the contours of their lives. Men do too. Allow yourself to recalibrate the scale of your needs and expectations based on your partner, especially if she is your priority and has a big place in your life. If you don't, it is emotional sabotage.

I call American men the "ATM of love." You tend to give love in many directions without prioritizing it. That is your primary faux-pas. The love for friends and hobbies shouldn't be equal to that of your partner and your children.

It seems many American women erect walls of protection when they are unclear of the "signals" that you give them. If you feel ready to be in, then be all in. Similarly, you have every right to take a step back if the relationship is moving too fast. You both deserve partners who are truthful about how they feel regardless of what those feelings may be.

Be aware that women compare the past to the present in silence. You must have many moments of self-evaluation and be on top of your game to be the partner she is looking for. The topics in this book are the ones American women are bringing to light. The choice is yours whether you wish to listen to what they are saying and make the efforts needed to be a good partner—not just a good man.

I wish you all happiness.

Bonne chance!

ENDNOTES

In Sickness and in Health

1   (pg. 4) Fred Hutchinson, Cancer Research Center. "Men Leave: Separation And Divorce Far More Common When The Wife Is The Patient." ScienceDaily. www.science-daily.com/releases/2009/11/091110105401.htm (accessed June 24, 2022).

2   Ibid.

3   (pg. 5) Evene.lefigaro.fr, accessed June 25, 2022, http://evene.lefigaro.fr/citation/amour-preuves-amour-1070.php.

How Was Your Day?

4   (pg. 9) Citation Célèbre, *Le Parisien*, accessed June 25, 2022, https://citation-celebre.leparisien.fr/citations/138889.

Bathroom Etiquette

5   (pg. 22) Britannica, T. Editors of Encyclopaedia. "Newton's laws of motion." Encyclopedia Britannica, July 23, 2021. https://www.britannica.com/science/Newtons-laws-of-motion.

Wives in Bad Marriages

6   (pg. 26) "Citation du Jour," *Ouest-France*, accessed June 25, 2022, https://citations.ouest-france.fr/citation-pythagore/mariage-seule-guerre-cours-laquelle-80701.html.

Excessive Drinking

7   (pg. 27) "Alcohol Use in the United States," National Institute on Alcohol Abuse and Alcoholism, March 2022. https://www.niaaa.nih.gov/publications/brochures-and-fact-sheets/alcohol-facts-and-statistics.

8   (pg. 28) "Figaro Scope", *Le Figaro*, accessed June 25, 2022, http://evene.lefigaro.fr/citation/hommes-noyes-alcool-mer-12050.php.

Erection Goes to Pot

9   (pg. 30) "Smoking & Tobacco Use," Centers for Disease Control and Prevention, March 17, 2022. https://www.cdc.gov/tobacco/data_statistics/fact_sheets/index.htm.

10   (pg. 30) "Marijuana and Public Health," Centers for Disease Control and Prevention, June 8, 2021. https://www.cdc.gov/marijuana/data-statistics.htm.

11   (pg. 30) Kovac, J R et al. "Effects of cigarette smoking on erectile dysfunction." *Andrologia* vol. 47,10 (2015): 1087-92. doi:10.1111/and.12393.

12   (pg. 30) Payne, Kelly S et al. "Cannabis and Male Fertility: A Systematic Review." The Journal of urology vol. 202,4 (2019): 674-681. doi:10.1097/JU.0000000000000248.

13   (pg.30) Harvard T.H. Chan School of Public Health, "Marijuana smoking linked

with higher sperm concentrations." February 5, 2019. https://www.hsph.harvard.edu/news/press-releases/marijuana-smoking-sperm-counts/.

14   (pg. 30) Hehemann, Marah C. et al., "Evaluation of the Impact of Marijuana Use on Semen Quality: A Prospective Analysis." *Therapeutic Advances in Urology*, (January 2021). https://doi.org/10.1177/17562872211032484.

15   (pg. 30) Feiby L. Nassan et al., "Marijuana smoking and markers of testicular function among men from a fertility centre." *Human Reproduction*, (February 5, 2019): Pages 1-9, https://academic.oup.com/DocumentLibrary/humrep/PR_Papers/dez002.pdf.

Take Initiative

16   (pg. 34) Citation Célèbre, *Le Parisien*, accessed June 25, 2022, https://citation-celebre.leparisien.fr/citations/20706.

Men and Condoms

17   (pg. 35) Joe Hernandez, "California is the 1st state to ban 'stealthing,' nonconsensual condom removal," *NPR*, October 7, 2021, https://www.npr.org/2021/10/07/1040160313/california-stealthing-nonconsensual-condom-removal.

18   (pg. 36) "Sexually Transmitted Disease Surveillance 2019," Centers for Disease Control, last updated April 13, 2021. https://www.cdc.gov/std/statistics/2019/foreword.htm.

19   (pg. 36) David Fincher, Director. *Fight Club*. Twentieth Century Fox. 1999. 139 minutes.

Strong Women

20   (pg. 44) Citation Célèbre, *Le Parisien*, accessed June 25, 2022, https://citation-celebre.leparisien.fr/citations/148471.

Cocky Confidence

21   (pg. 46) Citation Célèbre, *Le Parisien*, accessed June 25, 2022, https://citation-celebre.leparisien.fr/citations/47662.

Suggestion Box

22   (pg. 51) Citation Célèbre, *Le Parisien*, accessed June 25, 2022, https://citation-celebre.leparisien.fr/citations/42657.

Your GPS Won't Help

23   (pg. 55) Shaun Wooller, "Nearly half of men can't correctly identify a vagina," *The New York Post*, August 31, 2017. https://nypost.com/2017/08/31/50-of-men-cant-correctly-identify-a-vagina/.

24   (pg. 55) Herbenick, Debby et al. "Women's Experiences With Genital Touching, Sexual Pleasure, and Orgasm: Results From a U.S. Probability Sample of Women Ages 18 to 94." *Journal of Sex & Marital Therapy* 44, no. 2 (2018): 201-212. doi:10.1080/0092623X.2017.1346530.

25   (pg. 55) Julie Compton, "The 'orgasm gap': Why it exists and what women can do about it," *NBC News*, April 6, 2019. https://www.nbcnews.com/better/lifestyle/orgasm-gap-why-it-exists-what-women-can-do-about-ncna983311.

Body Shaming

26   (pg. 57) "Get The Facts," National Organization for Women, accessed June 27, 2022. https://now.org/now-foundation/love-your-body/love-your-body-whats-it-all-about/get-the-facts/.

Dating Women with Children

27   (pg. 62) "Stories: A Daugher's A Daughter,"AgathaChristie.com, accessed June 25, 2022. https://www.agathachristie.com/stories/a-daughters-a-daughter.

Male G-Spot

28   (pg. 70) Citation Célèbre, *Le Parisien*, accessed June 25, 2022, https://citation-cele-bre.leparisien.fr/citations/135042.

Gaslighting

29   (pg. 74) Jessica, "Stop Aux Pervers Narcissiques: Tout Ce Qu'Il Faut Savoir," *FemmedInfluence*, July 30, 2019. https://femmedinfluence.fr/stop-aux-pervers-narcis-siques/.

Religion

30   (pg. 78) Citation Célèbre, *Le Parisien*, accessed June 25, 2022, https://citation-cele-bre.leparisien.fr/citations/197603.

Relationships Are Doomed without Respect

31   (pg. 82) Evene.lefigaro.fr, accessed June 25, 2022, http://evene.lefigaro.fr/citation/colere-emplit-coeur-laisse-langue-aboyer-vain-11613.php.

Fathers of Daughters

32   (pg.88) Dico-Citations.com, accessed June 25, 2022. https://www.dico-citations.com/tout-homme-porte-en-soi-une-image-de-la-femme-qui-lui-vient-de-sa-m-re-c-est-elle-qui-le-d-termine-nietzsche-friedrich-wilhelm/.

Porn King

33   (pg. 90) Michael Malcolm, George Naufal, "Are Pornography and Marriage Substi-tutes for Young Men?" *IZA Discussion Paper No. 8679*, November 2014. https://crypto-me.org/2014/12/phlap-v-marriage.pdf.

34   (pg. 90) Kelsey Clark, "Pornography addiction: another reason for the U.S. marriage decline." *The Herald-Times*, January 27, 2015. https://www.heraldtimesonline.com/story/lifestyle/2015/01/28/pornography-addiction-another-reason-for-the-us-marriage-de-cline/47758627/.

Living With Your Parents

35 (pg. 92) Citation Célèbre, *Le Parisien*, accessed June 25, 2022, https://citation-cele-bre.leparisien.fr/citations/209743.

Climaxing

36 (pg. 99) "Female orgasm: No climax with vaginal penetration?" *Mayo Clinic*, ac-cessed June 25, 2022. https://www.mayoclinic.org/diseases-conditions/female-sexual-dys-function/expert-answers/female-orgasm/faq-20058215.

Generosity

37 (pg. 102) Citation Célèbre, accessed June 25, 2022. https://citation-celebre.lepari-sien.fr/citation/generosite.

Online Dating Dos and Don'ts

38 (pg. 103) Micheal J. Rosenfeld, Reuben J. Thomas, Sonia Hausen, "Disinterme-diating your friends: How online dating in the United States displaces other ways of meeting." Proceeding of the National Academy of Sciences, Vol. 116:36, September 3, 2019. https://doi.org/10.1073/pnas.1908630116.

39 (pg. 103)

40 (pg. 104)

41 (pg. 104)

42 (pg. 106) "Victims of Sexual Violence: Statistics," Rape, Abuse & Incest National Network, accessed June 25, 2022. https://www.rainn.org/statistics/victims-sexual-vio-lence.

Just the Tips

43 (pg. 124) Citation Célèbre, accessed June 25, 2022, https://citation-celebre.lepari-sien.fr/citations/79754.

44 (pg. 136) Maureen O'Hare, "Does being bilingual make you sexy?" *CNN*, April 2, 2017. https://www.cnn.com/travel/article/multilingual-language-benefits/index.html.

CPSIA information can be obtained
at www.ICGtesting.com
Printed in the USA
BVHW081050230123
656900BV00002B/93

9 798218 053581